I0153921

the deering hour

the
deering hour

Karen
Elizabeth
Bishop

ORNITHOPTER PRESS   PRINCETON

Copyright © Karen Elizabeth Bishop
All rights reserved

First Edition

Published by Ornithopter Press
www.ornithopterpress.com

ISBN 978-1-942723-11-0

Library of Congress Control Number: 2021943507

Cover image:
Panel for a Screen: Woman with a Deer (detail)
by Albert Pinkham Ryder
courtesy of the Smithsonian American Art Museum

Design and composition by Mark Harris

Contents

_____

_____

the deering hour

honeyhive

ghost says i unholding swarm
leaves a beehive unmounted i

        choose slope, pitch the pend,
        knucklegrass and kneebend,

bees everywhere like eyes
singing. the sky against the

        skull at the hard angle open
        cracks, yeses blind now the

hum a bloodthinner the
sun a boxcutter, it shuts

        down by silver hinge, thin
        wire discordant welcomed.

confession is built mouth
to open mouth until water

        wracked the sweet sacks stick
        reduced to god's-eyes opening:

i dilute you, you reduce me,
we build walls impenetrable

        that come undone in the hand,
        at the flame, on beating tongue

we consume what will not
hold, wordlike and storied.

answer answer

woolborn and battlespeak the stain says not shard not
sharp edge of sky unheard

      by

we fall we feel our way beyond the green trees follow
the shunt of light flowering

      toward

the field content does not describe but burns the structure
holds forth binds bone

      upon

bone like the call of the greylag one to the other i predict
i forewarn pull just here

      on

my neck a wish is a necklace that comes apart unclasped
hands at the throat catch

      at

desire that falls fast to the floor shimmering and gleaming
unpostulated untethered

      among

the weeds we rut here for grubs feed on sweetgrass and
waste the fat shining berry.

leaf-lung

we glacierlike breathe
　　against the green, abundance of leaf,
petiole storming, stamen
　　bronchioles. green in, green out, green
closed upon the branch.
　　alveolus fruit of the animal, leaf-lung a
fist that burns to spread
　　its slate eyes, the heartsea swells, the
wings like birds that do
　　not fly, the gaping, the brackbreath.

red

i exhibit red like a sea-change, flight unburied, a fiction of
          grammar unfurled like mossmeal on the skin. i read the
storm's path on my arms, a bright flesh-map of howling,
          bending, resistance from within. tall winds no one hears,

whistles that weave shrouds upon rock in waves of tumult,
          raw uprooting and forest scars that make welts on the back,
lacerations that measure time and mark the route of the buried
          river, tomorrow is a proposition not a promise. what difference

could be greater, algebra does not meet the sea head on, you
          will not last. the gesture that says, here i am stone, here i am
root is a bird whose feathers turn to back, doubting has an
          end, the certainty of flesh wears us out from within, the last

withholding the spine, the neck, the bird-sternum that holds
          back the call, cue-cue-cue, until madness sets in before the
mirror, beak to beak, breast to breast, your shining example a
          foil and a tongue, we rage against what we're not, confessed.

you were a house

for l.a.

you were a house of many rooms,
a stairwell, wainscotting. gladioluses

that came up through the floorboards
like flames. a house on fire, blooming,

haunted. soon the stalks fell burdened
with colour, bells pell-mell on the hall

planks. we collected them up. in that
house there were always footsteps on

the stairs, a light in the transom. you
were never empty, never alone. your

door always unlocked.

still to luminous

the mammal-moss does blossom sweet,
the sweet draughts come to naught. an
eye, an ear, the outline of what rots. this

is the place I touched your cheek, here a
lip unbent your face. untroubled, still to
luminous we went, in miles of downpour

we diluted what we meant. our hands a
pale translation of death yet shent, your
starry shoulder a corner of grief forwent.

luciferin

was it you or the foxfire
that gasped in the night?

interstellar

& there we were interstellar,
        prone, and paddled out to the middle
of the lake, two islands between us
        and the receding shoreline swamped
        with cattails and night frogs and the
corpse of one sunfish, belly up and swollen

just where the murky water turns to mud.
        so that coming down the yard toward
the dock, the air smells thick with garbage,
        but it's the stench of giving up that hangs
        heavy about the house, eyes bulging,
body arched skyward, oh just take me already

from these dark waters, I can't bear to look
        any longer upon these dark waters, oh
lord, take me before this night is through.
        release me from this void safe of passion,
        saved from the light of other eyes.
the murk of night, the silence, the knowing.

& we shored up beneath the heavenless sky,
        a kind of fiction afloat with four wet feet,
four hands busy with paddles that cut the water
        untroubled, undocumented, turned on its belly
        toward some greater force, unconcerned by our
gentle pleas to move forward, to advance, to arrive.

& we two black marks against the night shroud
        unfurled. a cry would not have broken through
its warp or weft, a cry would not have slipped
        through my fingers where I caught it with my
        looking mouth. I searched for you noiseless
at the edge of my teeth, your mouth inundated by dark

waters and unseeing eyes and by bare proximate
    blindness plunging into the night sky, here a
finger, yet here an arm, let me take you by the elbow,
    the slightest pressure and we'll turn here together
    like two birds in flight, the crooks of our wings
two right angles soaring toward some unnameable night.

horse or hare

what finally, is horse or hare, when texture gone,
when fingers recede and there's left the thing. oh
my mother has her secrets, i don't want to know
them, i've got mine. but there's touching and then

there's the sky. a kind of blessing, i think, to put
your hands back in your pockets, keep your head
down. not look up. shuffle past the stables closed
to snow, animals locked up for the night, hooks at

rest. the trees beyond speak of another warmth, of
other futures. new alphabets that test the tongue,
harden the heart, produce the window in the wall.
the way out is the way in, the door opened to the

thing untouched, observed, as white and bare as
milk in a metal bowl, grave to the fly who drowns
therein alive, gleeful with death face up, drunk at
having drunk the thing, become the thing, entered.

the deering hour

the moon's shadow does not
fall on our dividing line, our
way home is not eclipsed.
straight at the slant, here at the
heart, the road turns where
field becomes pitch, the hour
yields like plated gold clung to
the finger, here the surface
does not hold. where the final
hanging on comes to a close,
we are sound receding in
waves, four hearts quiet
ascending, the light at the
border dark increasing, the
light in the heart that beats
away at the margin of death,
we will not be murderers
tonight. the forest moves
forward, restless, black, half-
wild. the deering hour
advances in a straight line that
points us home, trees a
summer blizzard that hides the
animal heart, our knowledge
shallow and radiant, ignorant
and blindly beating it follows
to desire, chest forward, snout
out, hoof poised to make the
leap. stay, i say, stay, do not
jump, the sun is a vine that only
unwinds. but then aren't we,
too, rooted beasts who make
our way to some animal

destination, rut in the gouge,
scratch at the dirt, we build
windows. home turns our flesh
to stalk, we plant   ourselves,
meat-weary, we take the risk.
we will not die for it tonight,
but hold our breath and wait,
gold-stricken, bark- thwarted,
release-restrained, we look, we
measure: here our freedom,
here the shovel brings up bits
of bone, we choose neither nor
stray, we risk the wild to stay.

inflorescence

for l.s.

the drivinglight that parts your heart,
froststricken and savaged, two shadows
abate where gold is goneforth for a blood
murmur, youareyouareyouareyouareyou—

    decreation is an empty field where tall
    grasses take root

not every remembering happens at the edge
of lipsyllable, sometimes the tongue swells to
fill the whole mouth, the whole lung, a bird
aloft as the downpour clears, brightshining

    their feet like fingers in the dirt unstinging
    leaves shake free

you didn't say if you gave over, a last present
amidst our famine, or if you sought the wild
wasting of our white nights, the pleading scar,
fingers in the welt, the searing blightburn. and

    the hush and sway of the awn and glume,
    uncultivated, glad

snow edge

let this be home, where death does not
mean more than to swallow a mouthful
    of water,

easy-like, casual, tame. not the wild look
of brambles or trying to rid the heart of
    sun stroke,

but the clarity of a lost name recalled, yes,
the quiet candor of a surprise night-bone,
    white wake.

the firebreak holds the woods back from
going forward, the firn stops the snow
    from falling,

the middle names the thing, but the end
means it most sincerely. like this: look,
    it's snowing,

the trembling paused, leaves stilled, it
comes down without cause, constant,
    unconcerned

with contrast or choice, absolute. when
it stops, the snow edge of things, the blue
    that blinds.

after death, love the

rocks on the altar
like fallen stars
friends stop by to
check in, wonder.

griefs turn over in
the night, swollen
with bloat. love the
water that bears them.

an offering to small
gods: a whistle, a bell,
two hands to hold you
like salt on the tongue.

february

snowburst, for watersake   torrent
roofside slid, nothing else   but
white on white surrender   to the sun
now riverborn, free, burnt   [   ]
a cathedral of needles and   shade
on the slope where siltslip   swells.

only waiting outlives for   getting

lost we have the spring.

the last dogwood

forsythia, with what foresight do
you predict the spring? what turns
in the soil beneath you, what taps
at your roots that tells you, here
now the sun, here now the equal
night?

far amongst the oaks the dogwood
blossoms, just shy of the creek that
cuts along the gasline, trench to
herons and young deer who toss
heavy heads bearing new branches
and wanting.

the quiet comes in waves, before
the dark but after the spring sun
descends. we can't see a week out,
and beyond that not a month or a
summer. for now a pause, the still
born bloom.

at the pasture break

cow-grass spilt like stars overheav'n, split
at the mouth bruised and purple and small,
gives off the dank smell of honey uncollected
and creeping across the low field, a sharp jab of
hoof and mire, cuddochs turning in patches to
make of mud a home and a sweet place to rest.
while beyond the fence the forest dais'd, woods
that died a hundred years past, still the pines
stick straight like matches in the tinderbox, they
await the fire to take them home and clear the
land for fog, for newts that chewing through
prepare the charred ground for new growth and
green things. the blately rain comes in, soft the
undervoice to the sounds of things striving, the
conquering mosses and the linnet song, the meatly
earth swollen with new water and unspoken gruse.
like watching the world come in, clevering up over
the meadows and pitch rocks. cannae turn your back
to it so in you go, braindging and bleating and
beating about. we noisy spoilt spoiling things raising
muck and hirpling along while the grasses and creatures
take the measure of the quiet earth and slope accordingly.

○

the art of waiting

Yo no sé de pájaros,
no conozco la historia del fuego.
Pero creo que mi soledad debería tener alas.
—"La carencia," Alejandra Pizarnik

the way the rain goes,
the shunts of water
as i walk to the letterbox
and wait for your death.

i wait for it everywhere.
i held it, but i don't see it,
he said, the red bird at the
window trying to get in.

i don't know much about
birds, i don't know the
history of fire. but water
knows the art of waiting.

learning to swim

if your body if your brother if the water snaps
violence of the leaf upon the tree

& shudder etc. shroud

when you carry him across that ground sunlight
does not touch water

in eddies at your feet

unstabled like two black horses trapped by rocks
in the riverbed uplifted

overturned a catastrophe crossing over

the history of helplessness is the wish for lyric
song that makes religion little cuts in the dirt

slashes Xed into morning bread inside the thigh

a pocket opened and upon the palm a thirst:
learning to swim should cure dehydration.

blood plum

beyond the point where I am gone, he is not born with a caul
but with his lifeline wrapped twice around his neck, pulsating

like a toad's throat in summer fat with winter blood and milk,
calm and steady, loud. please don't tie me down I whisper and

you wink, nod, thin blade glinting in the bought light, I crucified
you open me upon a table and I don't feel a thing. later he will

wrap his finger around your finger first while they rearrange my
guts and my milk surges, a tide to meet you, the morning moon

rising to fall like a promise to your lips, I lie still. I've practiced
lying still before. like when I used to practice how to survive

the machine. arms tight at my side, not in the cross I will give
you as a name to bear you through the world, hands flat against

my thighs, the intersection slopes loose. I practice for hours, how
not to move, muscles in close corporation against the nerve like

flowers blooming to quell the twitching, think left, two fields over,
deny. but the wheel on the track does not sound, the hammers at

the skull, only pigeons springbound at the skylight, underwater is
hard to pretend. when they bring you to me I hold you like a plum

and have to fight the urge to bite into you, to take you back into me,
to pierce the thin skin with sure teeth like we used to, sour at first

then the surprise sweet flesh, cross-legged in the scant shade, backs
turned against the light to hoard the fruit against our kid mouths.

lily made of bones

lily made of bones, i didn't mean to grow fat. it happened by accident,
like a car crashes in the crossing that divides on the way from on the

way home. tires lock, we jump the curb, i understand it to be a fiction,
a dwelling. always a source of pleasure for the consideration of others,

from the back seat my flesh cries out. we leave a gash in the young
tree that emerges alone from the road, later evidence of our debt,

our ignorance, the whistling that accompanies the unseen end, the
cloud in the room, the pause. i wait for you to kick, but don't yet

imagine your broken nose, the black eye, the burn, your body a site
of inquiry you offer up freely, no expectation of recompense, no ask.

something now will pierce my body, i fold, but so does the sky with
me, you turn. they hook me up for hours to watch your heart beat, as

untroubled as a handful of wild blue phlox you grow, as free as a
fiery saxifrage, my son the stone-breaker, unbroken and whole,

content in your liquid universe to prepare the flint, mind the horses,
plot your escape, no thought for flesh or arms or how the flowers go.

girl in garden, portrait

after Bastien-Lepage

smoke and mirrors, you say, it's just a trick of the eye. but i
fall for it every time, i have fallen for it for years.

i want to give in every day for the rest of my life: the blank
space, the white smudge, the unknowing.

arms crossed, hips crooked, hand on your chin, you nod
toward the girl. do not go forward, i tell her.

turn around, go home. put on the water for your tea, mend
your dress. tend to your roses, put your hands

in the dark earth. predict the future from behind your garden
gate. but do not look. do not listen. do not go forth.

but her eyes are already burning, she's already lost to the light.
she hears them at her ear: go forth, go forth. speak his name

on your lips, trouble his name at your mouth. you will not feel
the pain at the end, it will not be more than words.

the pain will not be more than a bright light burning. and then
his voice: give me up to them. i will take your place,

you will not feel. give them the light, tell them: the light comes
in the name of the voice. give them my name, give

them silence. it's all smoke and mirrors, where the light hits the
eye there is no seeing. i don't understand the whites.

shells, you confess. shells, and shit, and flakes of lead left to sit
and rot and luminesce until properly applied it forsakes

all seeing. white is a face to the wall. no betrayal, no revelation,
nothing to see, the noise is terrible against the eyes.

knowledge comes fierce now, haunting always hard to watch.
the white smudge goes mute. your hands soften, we turn away

into the crowd. she listens at our backs, hands steady. she hears
the fire on the hill. the conflagration will last well into the night.

called back to salt

after Miller Oberman

called back to salt, sloughed off again in time, you stand knee-deep
in ocean ponds that gather

                        in leaps the body that left them behind

the door is yet open and light comes in relief, we don't see the brink,
the edge unbound beyond

                                  its borders bending sent

skin-riveted, absorbed we link our arms to cross the bridge, we two
sides of the city, you east and

                      i west, we vault into the air, outflung

we are not lost but unlost, not quite fully found, the sun squared
upon green water, against your

                           jaw &, the bell still rings &

the sky crumbles the city upon its girder, new roads ring the walls
that once marked the limits of

                      our openness, the unknown still forthwith

a city not planned but made and grew up around us like trees grow
wild upon the meadow plain,

                        turn left for the beating heart,

or maybe we go nowhere but make up patterns as we go, we think
we know the limits of our day-

                  making, night unmaking, certainty in a bridge

but everything wound will unwind and we with it as we draw our-
selves like string upon the road,

                      unriveted, skin-sloughed, bones and born

                    to the shining air.

types of meteors

1. aerial: hurricane, wind, your eyes

2. aqueous: rain, snow, ascension

3. luminous: aurora, arc, his hands

4. igneous: lightning, starshot, the fall

5. metamorphic: shock, impactite, the lintel

come

where you come from
does not mean me. zero

hour, white-eyed, redlorn.
for the oceanic, the shore

takes flight. like once i
lucid, breathcome shells

stalled, faltered. go at an
angle so the dune does not

come down beneath you.
footslopes breach our over

coming, like two straight
pines we come tidily apart.

the thin edge

not just her body, not just the site,
but the thin edge, the redwork that
tenses:

have you no shame, he asks, but
i don't understand the question.
so i take

a fifty-fifty chance, it could have
gone either way, like stars, said
no, no

shame at all. edge = to give an
edge to. edgehate. to urge on often
mistaken

for not just her body, but the thin
edge that means retreat without
exit

where the blood pools under the
skin and doesn't bloom purple
for days.

the history of flight

as she steps out onto the window's ledge
the traffic advances in fits and starts below

> the bowerbird practices metonymies of love and
> longing. he goes out collecting and brings home
> shells and leaves, feathers and stones, berries and
> branches. he organizes coins and nails, spent shot-
> shells and shards of coloured glass. from smallest
> to largest he lines them up so to force the perspective
> of she who will secure his survival. he mutters to
> himself like a crazy man as he builds his bower. he
> laughs like a pig while he dances. he hides behind
> the door and turns a blue eye on his lover as she passes

as she tucks her hair behind her ears
and smoothes her hands across her skirt

> a kaleidoscope of butterflies prepares to make its way
> from Mexico to the California coast where its number
> will hide amongst the dying blue gum eucs, hopeful
> wing turned to leaf in silver morning fog. a diapause
> upon the ocean branch while inland the super bloom
> grows wild in anticipation, lays down sheets in bright
> reds, oranges, yellows, bronze and the milkweed builds
> reserves to meet the coming demands of overwintering

as she takes a step forward and jumps
and the windows fast beside her recede

> bees drone overhead like a black cloud emerging on the
> weighted sky, they're coming for their queen mid-flight
> they give themselves over to her, abdomens ripped open
> tumbling sticky to the vast fields below, bodies rent

piled upon the grasses sweet with honey and desire.
the virgin spoilt shakes out her wings and hoards deep
within the nations she will birth. she decides from her
airborne throne: he will be a worker and she will be my
queen. so she writes her future and her end on the ignorant
air while the birds watch unconvinced and hungry

as she falls we all fall hers is the history of
flight the future of lyric the winter of our ash

little moons

and if the human cost should be collected
in some unexpected form:
                                    fingernails, say, or
                              orange peels. eyelids or
                                   irises in bloom.

                              yes, those broken flames in
                                    flower, towering
                         violets unabashed and doomed.

                              clippings from the paper or
                              hair or fingernails. verses or
                                   vespers or vying.

                                              yes,

and if the human cost of human life should
be collected in some
unexpected form:
                              measured in inhalation
                         and out again, the evensong, the
                                   bird upon the hill.

                              in flesh torn or undeliverable.
                              the glance. the lance. the will.
                              the open breast. recrimination.

                              or maybe fingernails. bone to
                                   skin or baby to breast.
                              two feet. water a weak behest.

                                              yes,

and if the human cost of laying waste
to human life should be collected in some

unexpected form:

                              hair. two eyes. a tooth.
                               the stones at your neck,
                      the carcanet. the knife undull.

                          as the edge of day presses
                  in at last to gut you from the side.
                         the glass, the task, two eyes.

                        like little moons upon a shelf,
                        bone to skin and skin to self.
                          just the tips, the very lips.

                        no blood was let. there's nothing
                                            to collect.

the bright spot

for my grandfather,
who killed a deer so his nazi prisoners could eat

if amongst you i see shadows
move like trees move against

the dimming sky green with
warning bending exhale move

inside now rains are coming
where shadows move amongst

you inside the forest a blur
beyond the window here is

wonder that appears bleak-
eyed eyes like pools of water

that do not see out the world
reflected where they look

what wonder when a colour
there a bright spot here oh yes

the world the world it has
not left me yet two fingers

linger at the throat a knot
yes the world remains hands

a tangle smooth upon the pants
come to rest on two knees that

knew once war the world upon
the brink a dark forest in the

foreign night the van a heap of
voices and huddling arms to

elbows to knees to lowered heads
on borrowed shoulders like a bow

a mass of men whose bodies
touch to confirm the world

they leave behind the hunger
like a claw the hollow of the

mouth a longing where want
cannot be met the empty hands

still they travel to the teeth like
antlers seeking touching the

night air still like ships sinking
after the evening storm a tentative

hoof an eye an ear turned toward
the west does not see the truck

come tumbling down headlights
low and furtive upon the coming

curve but he sees the head against
the trees the foot the broad ribs

stretched against the heart the quiet
closing of the lips the heavy tongue

the starving wonder is this body still
my body and they would kill him if

they could if they'd known he but
wore it in his name they hungered

where he did not for life the living breath
that might sustain he saw the beast intake

and leap leap into the headlong light
like an arrow from its arc arch into

the air he measured he aimed he mis-
took the road to strike the hart metal

and flesh combined and hoof where
tooth jaw to heart black lips distend

the death grimace paralyzed upon
the gutted mouth against the grate

the seeing eyes like pools of water
overflowed that do not see into the

light neck bloody with fur and red
flowers blooming his hand upon

the door he stalls the engine on the
clutch death rattle on the road each

one of them prey amongst prey
they would kill him if they hatred

a hunger fed by hunger a mass of
men and tendons and muscles

pulled taut on tender legs like shaking
stalks he leaves the door not shut

light like pools untouched upon
the road the beast needs a knife

skin pulled back to bare the moonlit
breast exhale two hands bent back

shove down make room he hands up
shoulder leg and spine four hooves

the prisoners they pass the body
along the floor free feet kicking ja

they nod ja hope a danger in the
eye they travel then the men and

beast into some dark forest to reach
a hidden camp war a stain upon

the night and built there a hearth
if not of peace of respite and cooked

the hindquarters in fire charred flesh
upon the lips hands clumsy with fear

they tear into the meat teeth trembling
and the soldier a jew he not yet

converted for a woman who would
give him no children but lend him

three and borrow his one the night
still young enough to see the weary

hunger on the bone a gnawing
that persuades all manner of

execution but first the gift of
a meal meat on the bone eat

go ahead please eat i espied
beneath the dark leaves this beast

he paused i struck i killed him
for you a gift so you may eat

we'll keep the fires going eat
the fires will yet burn eat you

will know flame and carnage
eat for now feel the beast at

your mouth let it lend you the
life i took may it give you life

may you find comfort in this
night no the world it has not left

me yet yet may i make wonder
with these two hands entangled

oh yes here the world the colour
the bright spot the knot at the throat

come home

come home to my photo on the wall,
my eyes a second, more alien blueness.
no grave necessary, death not quite yet,
i have tried for as close to kindness, a

thing rich in colour, birds. i will have
failed at sky, at the hour commences
now. yet from my new blue grave listen
for an arm, a leg, a whistle for thought.

the varieties of silence are still many
long before life delivers up the flesh to
ground, still long before we look out,

surprised and taken to hear so many
secrets broken, see so much distant
blue, feel the gaze freeze on the stair.

taking stock

day 126 of lockdown

no the tangle, woodwrought & stalks,
    sun swollen like a tick burrowed into
the soft corner of our bare necks we scrape
    at skin to remove what cannot be

excised. later the raw parts will blister &
    i'll lick around the edges with a careful
tongue to clean the wounds of the grassland
    like you might be new again, before the

bloom, before we leant our whole bodies
    beyond the grassline where bodies aren't
meant to go, greedy we were for flesh, for a
    summer sweetness before the birds come

with their beaks, discerning where the flowers
    crumble to hot green dust on the floricane,
leave a hard faint fruit in their place. the mad
    chatter of speechless mouthspears and

clutching feet, we wonder wealth or death, too
    much or not enough, what can be ours under
this flashing sky, can we collect it up into a glass
    that all the way to the top might make us

jewel-rich among this empty feast, the table laid,
    the door unlocked, the lintel gleaming with
desire, plates heavy with thievery, the sloping field
    beyond the only body safe to touch, untangle,

the thick summer air the only air we breathe, our
    only common rain. hands to ourselves we grab
about the edges, try to transgress. pull up the corner
    of the canvas, beclaim the world, we live.

field notes from the biological station

i. geomancy

1. the magpie: one for sorrow, two for joy. no birds on this hill, but we turn our attention to great fortune besides.

2. we call it the devil's field. too many rocks to cross.

3. this next part implies the cold. your face will not be enough. sit alone and see if you can feel the direction of the whole wind against the rock.

4. just before the gulley a pile of tin cans and metal scrap. remains from the prison camp at the end of the war. the nazis didn't make it up here until almost the end.

5. we never find the crash site. instead we circle two wire reindeer pens and cross a dry riverbed. you instruct me in irrigation and salt. we prefer not to know what's lost.

ii. reindeer life

1. i cannot bear to see such tight landscape, he tells me, one arm still before the window. there is no room for them to move. no room to wander. twenty years later we are still on this question of space.

2. my mind is not a reindeer's mind. but i know that they have a turn in their mind. a turn to spring. the new growth takes them north.

3. they have a taste for lichen. but in the summer they trample this lichen they like and eat other green things and flowers. whatever flower you choose they eat it. and also the red berries that flood the fell.

4. they follow the winter into the wind. the winds are changing. they have to behave in time. time on the slope falls differently.

5. human beings are not such ecological animals. the reindeer has another logic.

iii. malla

1. the dogs sit on the prow. we sit below deck. there won't be anyone there to check passports. i forgot my money anyway and the clouds carry us over.

2. we look to the water to tell us what we already know. it's hard to look past the shadow of the mountain.

3. three countries claim this corner. and here a woman who has swum around all three. i have also studied the names of all the trees and flowers, she tells me bending. and i was glad to do so.

4. wooden boards keep our feet dry. the suture holds for now.

5. at the top a sleeping hut piled over with rocks. we add one rock more and do not lie down. rain falls beneath us and we descend.

iv. constellations

1. we thought they might give us the mountain to celebrate. but they kept it for themselves. we're a nation apart.

2. soil, rice, jam. i eat the soil and pull three rocks from my mouth. they could have been teeth.

3. the ice age recedes. the medusa succumbs to her burns.

4. i do not hear you for the water at your back. later i will be jealous at the water at your window, the angle of your roof. your beds in a line.

5. i buried my face in the soil but did not open my eyes. i do not play at death.

v. bird thoughts

1. we are the noise. we are looking through the noise. birds correspond to thoughts.

2. the sun doesn't leave the shadow. it's the plants. they know their own mind. the mushroom flowers across the screen.

3. i pull a woman from the water. white like the moon and as distant. she tells me: your future is now. our future is now. she breaks in two.

4. sound travels like a nerve on the spine. i collect it here, you say, showing me your copper wires and tree branches. can you hear it, can you hear anything? a clearing upon the hill. the lightning above the door.

5. hands flat upon the table. a smokescreen and a skull. the noise comes in waves in light against the sky. trees lit up like eyes upon the shore unblinking. we turn back toward the sensing dark.

this plant with teeth

this plant with teeth
flowers overjawing
mouth lips heaven-
ward turned like two
new deer in profile
against the treebank
suck young cheeks
toward the sky tendons
tight in advance of
the leap petals back
anther and filament
raised in relief this
morning i overflower
this morning i over-
flower this morning i
leap antlers blooming.

○

Kilpisjärvi

The flat stone, like all things at a distance, appears only in a field of confused structure in which connections are not yet clearly articulated.

—Maurice Merleau-Ponty, *Phenomenology of Perception*

I.

Sevilla – Amsterdam – Helsinki – Rovaniemi – Kilpisjärvi. Biological
Station.

Shoes off. Roll call. Rooms. Switch. Unpack. Dinner. Grounds.
Welcome. Groups. We are here to: white space. But it won't snow
until the day after we leave. September X.

We are here to, in this case form. Our several ways, selvage

Night one: lichen is verb and noun, action and result. Soil predicts cloud. Slope names the hollow branch against the skin. I will not be the only one to not say my name. But I will practice it over and over. On the bus, in my bed, on the mountain. It tastes like

_____.

Something about birds and Swedenborg. The machine world. Prophecies. I'll find a home there, copper wires and radio calls I can't make out. Biophemes I can't pronounce. Photochemical fixers that divine my future plant life. Wax drawn from water. But first, a hike up beyond the tree line. We sit with rocks, look for signs on the ground, in the air. We count berries, track scat, count mountaintops. I don't need to get to the end to know I'm already living my future.

But I don't know this yet the first night. Reciprocity will come up. Body to scale, hand to field, eye to height.

My skin breaks out in mosslife. Plant rage upon the body. Leaf-lung. Breathe through the world not in it.

Still, I'll be glad not to imitate the mammal. To have to be something I'm not. Perform. There's also the dirt. But I'm still back with the birds. They seem to be hooked up to a receiver.

Four months prior: Edinburgh, Barcelona, Venice. One month later: Baltimore, Santiago, Sevilla.

Not two years later: Lockdown, day 61. Two cardinals, a summer tanager, and three rose-breasted grosbeaks. The grassland bleeds birds. We navigate the inflorescence. We walk the bloom.

II.

We assemble. Materialism of the encounter. Later we will affix our latitude to our shirts. Overheard on the train: vital what? The material shines through, I think, the world shines through.

We walk north along the highway before crossing the road. Cut through the holiday caravans. Up the trail to the first fell, then we split. Others go higher, we go left. There's a certain pedagogy to it.

We sit apart. There's something on reboot that dissembles. But we look for the break: branch, fruit, bird. This move is absolutely distinct from X. Analytical reflection starts from &. Without which there would be no. In the absence of _____, I take notes. No reduction. We swallow the signs.

As we walk you speak of salt. I think of tombs. Appearance is not being, but the phenomenon. We never find them in any case. Others have seen them.

About those birds: absolute self-evidence and the absurd are equivalent. Lockdown, day 67: three jays, two mourning doves, a crow, two wrens, one cardinal. In the absence of evidence, then _____? But there's been talk of a hummingbird.

The only bird that can fly backward.

I read adventure in the sky but I hoard it. I am not immune from error. And I can't tell the difference between the divine and the divined. The thickness of the world. This world means: we are not concealed. I am optimistic.

III.

If latent lies the flat stone, like all things at a distance. The
connections are ours to make, even as we are not fully given over.

Thorning dress, bee man, brown paper sack. The whirl of the switch
pre-skin, before the light sets back in, the charge, the meaning.
Quiver. Where the air tenses, we wait. Charged. Precise
hold on the spectacle, etc. We place our confidence in the world, yet
adherence has a cost. Correction and recollection. &.

A hill unmarred by the stain of time. The mossworld makes its own
stain. Green on green, a flash of blue in the clearing. When I open
my mouth I can see them. Plosives are quieter. More animal.

In the grave sounds, immanence. I am not herd. Not either rock or
rain. I do not withdraw, but fall short of the world and think of other
slopes, other faults.

On a clear day, across to Morven and Scaraben. North laid out for the counting. Like sparks from a fire, one thrust, two, three. The push forward, being filled with wonder – for x, we move for x – and sometimes as far as Wick. But the horizon always seemed to me pure acoustics.

The sea divides us. A period of uplift and exhumation.

Transpressional displacements responsible for reactivation. A slip on the left pushes the right into action. To foresee means to: _____.

Appearance is the past. What misleads us in this connection is the illusion of an inner life, noisy and riveted within a world already spoken and speaking. The approaching future, the wilderness beneath the chatter of words, the bloom for dread.

The only thing we know about the future is X. Or if you plant-hands, bird-thinking, cloud-eyes, divination by salt. The wound leaves a mark in the belly of the bowl, this is where causality happens.

Oil sways where water bends. Just ask your question.

IV.

Not any present but sheer persistence which is beyond appearance, offering either x, y, z or only the earth.

I knew already how to sit with rocks. Poet: to pile up, build, make. But also: to shove, push away, thrust with violence. Uplift and exhumation.

No, leave the errata. They let the light in. The glacier less so.

We watch from the shore of the moraine as the future recedes. A noise like bones splitting. We record it from different angles and at different speeds, blink before the evidence. This is consistent with shallow burial. This is consistent with the orchid.

Someone devises an auroral alarm. Put a note on your door if you want to be woken up to see the lights. A mnenomic exercise.

Scale gives us intimacy. Two branches bearing fruit: take this apple either or the other. The sky comes in green waves like a door knocking. You go your way, I'll go mine.

The reindeer use the lights to navigate the mountain.

The fire at the heart rushes forth. This will taste of summer, she says. He is young, and has been grazing his way north for the past several months. He will taste of grass and wildflowers.

I haven't found my way yet. My name lingers in my throat. But I take you twice into my body.

We eat the metonym. We swallow the signs. Words like A = A go up in smoke. My symbiont north, while outside the sky circles the stone.

It will snow the day after we leave. We are unready.

V.

As for water, we tell stories. Something about a naked man who
bears a sceptre in his right hand, a whip in his left, a crescent crown.
He governs the liver. Engrave him on a stone of hematite, hide
vervain beneath, enclose both within a golden ring. Wear while
abstaining from songbird eggs.

When I arrive, you're recording radio signals. Pi is the time from

_____ to _____.

It doesn't belong to circles, it just happens to show up there. We can
hear the interface better if we string it with lights.

Sine is acceleration opposite to where you stand. I'm on the lower deck, level to the water. It changes speed. Saana moves away from Malla as we get closer. I don't want to dock.

Question: Why does depth strike us so? Or, why do we seek relief?

First reply (but this is not a reason): depth is not visible. The human eye does not perceive depth. There is no relief.

Second reply: I can't see depth because depth conceals itself point by point instead of appearing, peacock-like, in an array of world-becoming. There is also no vision. Vision is thought.

Third reply: Birds are thought. Space begins where birds end.

We stand under.

Rectification (or convergence): sometimes the world comes into relief. When it appears, there are more than just signs. Depth is movement. Depth is an exchange between:

end and chance means and choice substance and opportunity accident and prediction matter and resistance power and form body and we mind and us bird and sky.

A privileged state that wants what we want. The movement of our eyes (birds) and the three-dimensional look are reciprocally means and end (still birds). This is the space we inhabit.

You ask us to interpret the water. Depth emerges. The mountain gains on us. Here chance responds to choice.

Before ascending, we skirt the corner of the lake. Sine stalls. Our knowledge is a liquid trilogy. I want to get in. Float like a cross. Instead we rise.

Don't talk to me about eyes. I saw you ahead on the horizon of the hill. We'll begin with facts.

The edges of the world are not visible. The mountain is not one mountain. The suture does not hold. The way down does not come.

I don't want to mention just the mistakes, the dark room. It's also the smell the earth gives off when it rains: of wet duck, lilacs, women's hair. The distances that get narrower when the weather is about to change. This flatness of blood that sometimes heralds the snow or hail.

We do not catch the curve. The strange burning that alights in the field.

Prolepsis: relief exceeds our anticipation. The clouds below us break
into rain. We follow its outer shore to find our way back.

VI.

Pi is the unwavering space of the constant form. The blank space that
completes the circle between the further forth and this shore.

I carry the bird with me in my pocket for weeks. I like to think of.

Materials
1 raspberry pi. 1 picam NoIR. 1 USB power bank. Potassium nitrate.
Sugar. Copal tree sap. Nichrome wire. Motorcycle battery. Night sky.
Aurora borealis.

Instructions

1. Connect picam to raspberry pi.
2. Install dark2.py on raspberry pi.
3. Edit / etc. / rc.local to run dark2.py on reboot.
4. Place pi USB power bank in waterproof tray.
5. Attach USB power bank.
6. Tape picam to Perspex sheet (pointing upward, toward sky).
7. Tape up whole tray.
8. Leave for several days.
9. Using motorcycle battery, nichrome wire, and pine tree sap, attempt to re-enact auroral activity to provoke new visions.

The horizon is the hyperobject. I see birds. The tree line goes blank before throwing its door wide open. The line goes dead. The sky is on the move.

Appearance is not being, / but the phenomenon. / This opening upon a world / makes possible some distance away / a large moving shadow. / Our adherence to the X / enables me to X / at the expense of Y. / We are not immune from error. / Not of any one thing, / terror, the thickness of the world, / they are strictly contemporary. / The world gives me.

Isostatic readjustment may still be continuing. The beaches rise on.

Three faults and a thrust. There must be more. The exact timing and the causes of this reactivation are still uncertain.

But

sonic velocities   (your voice against the wind)
vitrinite reflectance   (the incident light)
apatite fission tracks   (damage trails)

confirm exhumation and uplift.

The plume is alive. We're moving.

VII.

That leaves sky.

VIII.

We believe the world. With no effort we break the bone of the void. The earth shows through.

The sign swallows up the movement. We raise timber, voice. We make to stay. We're not staying.

It's hard to think of orchids growing here. Some of us cross the road and hike up the side of the waterfall. The bones split at our back.

Catastrophe is blind. Untroubled. The incident light comes in slantwise, we watch our footing on the slope. But the tumult and the clamor do not resound. Our future is silent.

Anterior to any affirmation.

IX.

We step back. Eat soil. Swallow rocks. Give things names. Mark the date. Record. Arrange. Explain. Propose.

Once the break is made, it is irreparable.

The field endows the bright spot, the stone confirms the shadow. But self-evidence and _____ are mutually implicatory. Even indistinguishable.

I do not look for my hand in the dirt, nor my waist in the water. I do not say my name.

The faults align before the word, underfoot.

They rose like a flower to close Iapetus. The self-same shore a stalk of many petals. Home the flat stone, like all things at a distance.

The illusory stone is the bright spot. The stone on the path.

I wave your wand around, seek a message in the sound. I cast a figure on the water, stare past the glass, look for the lie. But the swallow moves the sign.

Between bird and branch, the sky. Between bird and bird, the sky.

Stone gains on sky as we make our ascent. We come out above the clouds (late Cambrian). We hear the ocean closing: slip / strike, slip / strike. The spine makes a bridge for walking.

Our near end is not more than a shallow place. We turn our backs to it.

Return to gather. We light the fires, draw circles on the ground. Offer reports and propositions. Lie on our backs and watch the inside night. Make questions out of sticks.

I joint words to grass, punctuate rain. Some bring berries and found things. Not more than a lake.

Chance is consistent with choice. Choice the violence of craft.

The rain soaks the verse. Under cover, we speak in surprises, measure the fell in objects and action. But the continuities we craft prove the break. Where a word, the world recedes. We are luminous, but the sun echoes elsewhere.

I want to walk alone above the hill. The incline gives us the indefinite integral. The incline gives us the orchid.

X.

The fjord and the firth are both lined with small pebbles. Tools of a rude calculus that confirm our future anterior to any affirmation.

The world is certain. Its parts are not.

We are strictly contemporary. Cenozoic.

Lockdown, day 72: The deer misjudges us. Leaps too soon, flowers over. No trace of blood on the car.

We cut a path for ourselves over the rocks. Come down the other side of the forest, arms raised. To live a thing is not to coincide with it.

When I perceive a pebble, &. The thing is not all of a piece.

XI.

The lake emerges from the night like a hand. Everywhere there are warnings with no one who issues them. Electricity breaks on the circumference, we listen for some indication, a pulse. We hold our breath, we have a world.

But rock does not distinguish between here and now. We are strictly. I am at grips. We cling forth.

In the space between the switch and the body, bird. Cleanse me of what I have desired, make me less. The substance of the colour: night-blinking, raw. I am constant against the dark relief, and in my inclination. But do not swim. Between the switch and me, the hand.

Opens.

Upon a world and an object, beyond the tools we make for ourselves. May even, snow melts.

The living present is torn between O = X. But faults and veins provide structural evidence. We are not concealed. The gesture abides. We risk it.

As I came around the curve, I saw you knelt at the water's edge. Counting the water, you said.

That night you helped me scan the silent air. Our future from across the hill, you said. I heard the light on the horizon, but it was bent. I was already packed.

XII.

Inverse operation. Night train prolongs the end. If I, &, we emerge to day.

In Helsinki, we lock up our luggage and make our way to the harbour. We sit at tables near the water and drink coffee with milk. Sine changes speed. A natural sway. We visit a room whose window gives out upon the way down. We follow it. Later we'll go to look together at waves, point up from our backs at the changing light.

With the evening, rain. In the flesh.

We sit under a glass roof.

○

Notes

"the quiet candor of a surprise night-bone, / white wake" recalls W.S. Merwin's "The Bones of Palinurus Pray to the North Star" from *A Mask for Janus*.

"the history of helplessness is the wish for lyric" is borrowed from Patrick Pritchett's "Beginning with a Line from Peter Riley" from *Song X: New and Selected Poems*.

"lily made of bones" borrows from John Taggart's monostich "My Flowers."

"called back to salt" borrows its title and several other fragments from Miller Oberman's "The Unmaking" from *The Unstill Ones: Poems*.

"the history of flight" was written in memoriam after visiting the 9/11 Memorial and Museum in Manhattan.

"little moons" was written in memoriam after the 2017 white supremacist terror attack in Charlottesville, Virginia.

"second, more alien blueness" is from Paul Celan's elegy for Paul Éluard, "In Memoriam Paul Eluard."

"Kilpisjärvi" reworks several fragments from Maurice Merleau-Ponty's *The Phenomenology of Perception,* translated by Colin Smith. "Materials" and "Instructions" were written by the Augury working group at the 2018 Bioart Society's Field Notes laboratory at the Kilpisjärvi Biological Station.

Acknowledgments

My thanks to the editors of *The Ekphrastic Review,* who published versions of "field notes from the biological station" and "this plant with teeth" in 2018 as part of a collection of writing from Finland's Bioart Society's art-science field laboratory *The Ecology of Senses,* held in Lapland in September 2018. I am indebted to the Bioart Society for funding the residency; particular thanks to Erich Berger, Hannah Rogers and the other members of the Augury and Second Order working groups for their kind and on-going collaborations. "Kilpisjärvi" responds to my time at the Biological Station.

Heartfelt thanks to Patrick Pritchett and Teresa Villa-Ignacio, the first readers of this book, for their generous conversations about its evolution and their unwavering enthusiasm for the project. Patrick, thank you for steadying my eye and my hand. My deepest gratitude to Mark Harris at Ornithopter Press, for his keen, constant support of the book, and for bringing it into the light.

And to Luis, Theodore, and Julian: *the deering hour* is for you. May we always be heading home.

About the Author

Karen Elizabeth Bishop is a UK/US poet, translator, and scholar. Born in Birmingham, England in 1972, she grew up along Scotland's Moray Firth and in Southern California. She has lived in Austin, Sevilla, Oakland, Santa Barbara, Paris, Boston, and New Jersey, and holds a B.A. in Literature from the College of Creative Studies and a Ph.D. in Comparative Literature from the University of California at Santa Barbara. Former Lecturer in History and Literature at Harvard, she is currently Associate Professor of Spanish and Comparative Literature and chairs the Critical Translation Studies Initiative at Rutgers University. Her scholarly work includes *The Space of Disappearance: A Narrative Commons in the Ruins of Argentine State Terror* (SUNY Press, 2020) and *Cartographies of Exile: A New Spatial Literacy* (Routledge, 2016). Her research has been supported by the École normale supérieure in Paris, the Office of the President of the University of California, the American Council of Learned Societies, and the Bioart Society of Finland. Current creative works include the book-length elegy *Winter, Burn* and a hybrid collection of pseudotranslation, essay, and original painting titled *Salt*. She is the publisher of Lampblack Press and divides her time between the wilds of New Jersey and Sevilla, Spain.

www.ingramcontent.com/pod-product-compliance
Lightning Source LLC
Chambersburg PA
CBHW031002090426
42737CB00008B/639